koko &roo

First Day Of School

Dedicated to the loves of my life, my precious family.
Giving God all the glory for this incredible opportunity.
My prayer is for this story to touch lives, connecting us worldwide as we're all on this journey together.

Hugs and kisses from Mummy and Daddy,
two little friends set off on an adventure.

The start of something new, it was the first day at school for Koko and Roo.

Excited and nervous, they walked to their class, eager to meet new friends and have play time on the grass.

This week's focus is all about the Fruits of the Spirit.
"But what does that mean?" asked Geraldine Giraffe.

Think of the prettiest tree you ever did see, began Teacher Tortoise, with all sorts of fruits beaming with glee. Each fruit represents something unique, guides to live by and ways to speak.

The first fruit we're talking about today, is love, we'll keep practising it until it fits like a glove. All the other fruits seem to join hand in hand, fitting perfectly the way it was planned.

We will find joy, peace, patience and kindness. Not forgetting the rest that is self-control, faithfulness, gentleness and goodness.

With all these fruits fresh on their minds, the bell rang for first play. Eagerly running out of the door, the children simply couldn't wait a minute more!

Pushing and shoving to get out first, one of the children was bound to be nursed.

"Have patience little ones!" Teacher Tortoise said with a loud burst.

Koko and Roo were filled with joy as they welcomed their new friend Lily Elephant, before the play's end. Teacher Tortoise was as pleased as could be, as he spotted a fruit between the three.

While playing hopscotch, Koko and Lily both seemed sad and cross. "What's wrong?" asked Roo. "We aren't as good as you," Lily quickly said.

"That's ok guys," said Roo, which was wise, "God made us all unique. I can help you with hopping today... let's get started and hop hop away! One day you'll teach me something new so I'll be able to learn from you."

Teacher Tortoise said well done to Roo.
"You showed wonderful patience and kindness, teaching Koko and Lily what to do. I'm immensely proud of you."

Roo blushed with gladness knowing he had helped with Koko and Lily's sadness.

"What does patience mean?" asked Danny Dingo...

"Patience means taking your time without getting annoyed. It can also mean staying calm and not rushing ahead. Remember practice makes perfect, no matter how long it takes. Besides, slow and steady wins the race.

How else can
we practice
patience?"
asked Teacher
Tortoise with a
smile.

The children took their seats at their desks.

“I know, I know!” said Lily while putting her trunk up.
“My Mommy tells me to have patience when I try something new, or when I’m learning to read and write.”

"Yes, that's quite correct Lily. We also need to have patience when learning to ride a bike, or playing with our little brothers and sisters too," said Teacher Tortoise.

“Teacher Tortoise, can we speak about kindness please?” asked Koko.
“Yes of course we can, would you like to tell me what you think kindness is all about?” asked Teacher Tortoise.

“Well in our family we believe that kindness flows from your heart; kind hands, and kind words to set you apart. Being kind is also about being soft and gentle, not being mean to others and helping out wherever you can,” said Koko.

”That’s wonderfully explained Koko, you are spot on! Being kind is a great attribute to have.

It shows that you love, you care and you understand,” said Teacher Tortoise.

The children settled in after their second play.

“Right class, we’ve spoken about most of the fruits, there’s just one left that can have nasty roots, it is called self-control.

Remember a little earlier when you rushed out for first play, you all seemed to be in each other’s way. Now had we shown some self-control, we could have all walked out in a nice little stroll.

See, self-control requires things to be perfected, like staying cool, calm and collected.

This may not always be an easy thing to do, especially when you're being corrected," Teacher Tortoise wisely explained.

"To conclude today's lesson, let's think about that pretty tree, with all the fruits beaming with glee - well you are the tree and all these beautiful attributes are fruits we would like to see.

With daily efforts and a little grace, developing your fruits is the best starting base.

Love, joy, peace, patience and kindness, self-control, faithfulness, gentleness and goodness... all of these things are in your reach, all it takes is to practice what you preach.

Now to end off our day in the best possible way, let's close our eyes as we pray.

"Dear God,
Thank you for loving us and creating us all unique. We ask that you would guide us in developing our fruits each week. Help us to try our best, so we can show others what it means to be blessed.
Amen"

Spot & Count

1 x Koko
1 x Roo

3 x Lily
4 x Danny

3 x Teacher Tortoise
2 x Geraldine
15 x The cross

School

Recap Questions:

- What does it mean to love someone?
- Why was Teacher Tortoise proud of Roo?
- What does patience mean?
- How can you be more patient?
- How can we show kindness with our family and friends?
- What do we call being cool, calm and collected?
- How can we develop our fruits?
- What's the best possible way to end off the day?

The Fruit of the Spirit is a biblical term that makes reference to nine attributes of a person, found in Galatians 5:22-23 "But the fruit of the Spirit is love, joy, peace, patience, kindness, goodness, faithfulness, gentleness, and self-control."